SCRAPPY DUOS

COLOR RECIPES FOR QUILT BLOCKS

DONNA LYNN THOMAS

Martingale
& COMPANY

BOTHELL, WASHINGTON

Scrappy Duos: Color Recipes for Quilt Blocks
© 2000 by Donna Lynn Thomas

Martingale & Company
PO Box 118
Bothell, WA 98041-0118
www.patchwork.com

That Patchwork Place is an imprint of Martingale & Company.

Printed in Hong Kong
05 04 03 02 01 00 8 7 6 5 4 3 2 1

Library of Congress Cataloging-in-Publication Data

Thomas, Donna Lynn
    Scrappy duos : color recipes for quilt blocks / Donna Lynn
Thomas.
        p. cm.
    ISBN 1-56477-307-8
    1. Patchwork—Patterns.   2. Quilting—Patterns.
I. Title.
TT835.T435 2000
746.46'041—dc21
                                                                00-033933

MISSION STATEMENT

We are dedicated to providing quality products and service by working together to inspire creativity and to enrich the lives we touch.

CREDITS

President · Nancy J. Martin
CEO · Daniel J. Martin
Publisher · Jane Hamada
Editorial Director · Mary V. Green
Editorial Project Manager · Tina Cook
Technical Editor · Ursula Reikes
Copy Editor · Karen Koll
Design and Production Manager · Stan Green
Text Designer · Trina Stahl
Cover Designer · Stan Green
Illustrator · Laurel Strand
Photographer · Brent Kane

DEDICATION

This book is dedicated to the men in my life—my beloved husband, Terry, and my two fine sons, Joseph and Peter, who have become young men of whom we are exceedingly proud.

ACKNOWLEDGMENTS

I RECEIVED AN awful lot of help bringing this book to print. An incredible number of quilting friends made the beautiful quilts found in the gallery. They took the book concept and block assembly instructions and made quilts with no additional help from me. Some had so much fun, they asked to do more. The result is an inspiring collection of unique designs and proof that the idea is fun and it works!

I owe a world of thanks to Kari Lane, Jo Wright, Merri Wright, Kim Pope, Ann Woodward, Robin Chambers, Deb Rose, Cathie Yeakel, Karen Reed, Linda Kittle, Linda Harker, and Dee Glenn.

Of course, my own quilts would never make it into my books if I couldn't call on some wonderful quilters who bring them to life with their quilting skills. Big debts of appreciation are in order for Kari Lane, Judy Keller, and Ann Woodward for their beautiful work.

As always, I owe a great deal to the tireless and exceptional technical editing skills of my friend and editor, Ursula Reikes. We work so very hard to produce error-free books!

One final thank you goes to my friend, Sally Schneider, for her conceptual contributions to this book. It would not be as full an idea without her input!

CONTENTS

INTRODUCTION

I LOVE SCRAP QUILTS! In my mind, the more prints in a quilt, the merrier. I delight in the visual feast of a scrappy quilt full of a wealth of prints and colors. It makes my heart sing to sit on the floor and play with my stash strewn all around me like an explosion while planning my next scrap quilt.

Too often scrap quilts seem muddy or brown in tone, not because those are the colors chosen but because that's how the eye blends the colors together. I don't like that muddy look and so, years ago, set out to find a way to make delicious scrap quilts that enabled the prints to shine on their own without blending into a brown mush.

"Birds in the Air" by Donna Lynn Thomas, 1992, Dorf-Guell, Germany, 51" x 59½".

I devised an easy, structured approach to making my beloved scrap quilts while planning the "Birds in the Air" quilt found on the cover of *Shortcuts to the Top* (a book of mine that is now out of print). I knew that if I colored every triangle in each block with a different dark or light print, as is generally done when making scrap quilts, the end result would most likely be brown. It occurred to me as I planned "Birds in the Air" that I could better showcase each print in the quilt by cutting all the pieces for one block from just one dark or medium print and one background print. By using a different set of dark and light prints for each subsequent block, I'd still end up with a dazzling array of prints, but each set would shine in its very own block. I call this a rainbow recipe and, as you can see, the finished quilt really sparkles.

As I was writing the cutting and assembly instructions for "Birds in the Air," I realized that each block called for an odd number of dark half-square triangles. Since I rotary-cut pairs of half-square triangles from squares of fabric, I decided it would be more efficient to cut two blocks from one set of prints. By doing so, I could cut an even number of triangles (six instead of three) from three squares of fabric and avoid leftovers. Thus was born the concept of making scrap quilts a pair of blocks at a time. You will find this duo approach to scrap quilts scattered throughout all of the books I have written since then: *Stripples, Stripples Strikes Again!*, and the revised versions of *A Perfect Match: A Guide to Precise Machine Piecing* and *Shortcuts: A Concise Guide to Rotary Cutting*.

There are many other benefits to this approach beyond the fact that you get to use lots of prints. First, choosing just a few fabrics for one pair of blocks at a time is a manageable task for anyone, whether beginner or advanced. This is a key consideration because it eliminates the trepidation and confusion many quilters experience when trying to figure out just where and how to start planning a scrap quilt with a multitude of prints. You need to concern yourself with the fabrics for and cutting of only one pair of blocks at a time.

Second, it's not necessary to cut out the entire quilt all at one time. I find the task of cutting an entire quilt daunting and time consuming, and procrastinate horribly when faced with such a big job. However, if it's just a pair of blocks, I eagerly dive in, pick some fabric, and cut and sew a pair of blocks in no time at all. It's just one more reason I love making quilts this way.

Your scrap quilts can be "built" as slowly or quickly as you like—a pair of blocks at a time. Each time you make a new pair, your pile of blocks quietly grows in the corner until one day you find you have the number needed for your quilt. This is quiltmaking for busy people, accomplished in a structured, small-bits-of-time, yet progressive manner.

One bonus to this pair-of-blocks-at-a-time approach is that you don't need large quantities of any one print to make these quilts. It is rare to need more than a fat quarter each of two or three prints to make a pair of blocks. (Most often you need even less than that.) Also, consider the fact that you don't have to buy the fabric for a whole quilt up front. Along with using what you have on hand, you can augment your prints by trading with friends and buying small cuts of special fabrics as you find them, thus spreading the expense out over a period of time. And remember, since you don't closely match fabrics as you would with a fixed palette of prints, anything goes.

Another fun aspect of this approach is the interesting overall designs created by setting blocks straight without sashing. This works quite nicely with a single block repeated and set straight as in "Birds in the Air." But you also have the option of taking the block interplay one step further by alternating two different blocks in the same quilt to come up with some really dazzling quilts. The play on two at a time becomes multilevel at this point—two block designs, each assembled two at a time, each pair from a different set of prints.

In addition to the rainbow recipe discussed earlier, you can use other methods to color your quilts. In a color-family recipe, you assign a color family to each position in a block and then follow that recipe for each pair of blocks you make. For instance, you could use red, blue, and gold as your color-family recipe and color each pair of blocks with a different set of red, blue, and gold prints. This very popular approach provides more consistency from block to block while still maintaining the excitement of a scrap quilt.

Your scrap quilts can be "built" as slowly or quickly as you like—a pair of blocks at a time. Each time you make a new pair, your pile of blocks quietly grows in the corner until one day you find you have the number needed for your quilt.

A mixed recipe combines a little of each of the two other approaches in one quilt. For example, you could assign a color family to one or more positions in one of the block designs and let the rest of the positions be a rainbow of colors. Or you could assign color families to all the positions except one and let that one position be a wild card color in each block. The choice is yours when planning your quilt. This approach can help tie the blocks together more tightly without being as controlled as a color-family recipe. This is especially desirable if you are interested in emphasizing a diagonal line or secondary design that you may discover in the blocks you've chosen. All of these options are discussed in greater detail later.

This book will teach you how to design your own unique quilts, plan your fabric choices, and then complete the quilt. There are no instructions given for the quilts pictured in the book. However, with the design tools and step-by-step instructions provided, you will find an unlimited number of quilts to make and the confidence and know-how to see them through to completion.

To this end, you will find twenty 12" finished blocks, each with complete cutting and assembly instructions for a pair of blocks. In addition, I have provided pages of shaded cluster drawings for each block that you can photocopy, cut, and paste onto a master quilt grid to design your own unique quilts. There are also unshaded block cluster drawings that will help you custom color your color-family or mixed-recipe quilt designs.

I hope to introduce you to an exciting new way to design glorious, exciting scrap quilts in a structured and comfortable format. As you flip through the many color samples and ideas in *Scrappy Duos*, you'll find your fingers itching to start sewing. Once you get started, you'll be surprised at just how much fun it is to create these dazzling quilts!

DESIGNING YOUR QUILT

SCRAPPY DUOS QUILTS are exciting quilts made from a variety of fabrics and one or, more often, two different blocks set together alternately without sashings. This creates quilts with fascinating secondary overall designs formed where the different blocks meet.

The duos concept works on a second level since you make blocks two at a time using a different set of prints with each repeat. The result is a scrappy quilt without the confusion of trying to work with lots of prints all at once. The block assembly instructions that begin on page 42 give directions for making just two blocks. Make all subsequent pairs of blocks using a new and different set of prints. Continue making as many pairs of blocks as your particular quilt requires.

There are no directions for actual quilts in this book since the idea is for you to come up with your own creations. There are lots of finished quilts and drawings provided for inspiration. On page 41 you will find a gallery of the blocks from which all the quilts featured in this book were made. Please note that all the blocks have a finished size of 12".

GETTING STARTED

To DESIGN your quilt, you need to have the block clusters beginning on page 84 and the master quilt grid on page 94, sharp paper scissors, a set of colored pencils, a gluestick, access to a copy machine, and your sense of adventure. Try to find the new removable gluesticks if you can. The glue in these sticks is not permanent. Instead, you can position, lift, and reposition your design as you make changes.

Once you have gathered the supplies, browse through "Gallery of Blocks" and pick out several blocks that you like and think would work well together in a quilt. Look for blocks with interesting corners that would connect well with others. Or choose blocks that have a diagonal feature that creates visual interest when paired with other blocks. If you choose two blocks that have squares or triangles that meet at the outer corners, remember that those four corners will not form one large mass. You'll get a four-patch unit instead, since each piece will be made of a different print.

Once you have selected your blocks, turn to the block clusters beginning on page 84 and find the appropriate blocks. Each cluster is a repeat of one block that you can photocopy and cut apart. Be sure to do a test of a page to make sure you can see the shading clearly. If you can't, lighten or darken the setting on the copy machine as neces-

IF YOU HAVE TROUBLE deciding which blocks to use, I suggest you make three copies of each cluster page so you have an ample selection of blocks from which to pick and choose as you play with ideas. Cut them apart and bag them. Label the bag. You now have a complete set of blocks to make any quilt possible. This is also a good idea if the copy center is not conveniently located just around the corner. You make only one trip. Don't forget to make ample copies of the master quilt grid while you are there.

sary. Since each cluster contains six blocks, you shouldn't need more than two or three copies of any one cluster. Notice that each block has a shaded and unshaded cluster version. The shaded blocks help you design your quilt, while you will use the unshaded blocks later to color your final quilt design. You will also need to make several photocopies of the master quilt grid on page 94.

Once you have made your copies, cut your shaded and unshaded block clusters apart. Place each group of blocks into individual resealable plastic bags and label them with the block name. This will keep the blocks from getting lost, especially if you have cats!

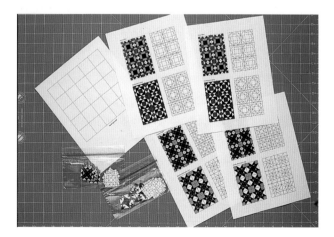

CUSTOMIZING YOUR QUILT GRID

THE MASTER quilt grid on page 94 is a 5 x 5 layout because this is enough blocks to see a design take shape and still fit within the space limitations of a book. Since all the blocks in the gallery have a finished size of 12", a 5 x 5–block quilt would be 60" square without borders. You are not restricted to making a quilt of that size, nor are you restricted to making a square quilt. If you want a smaller quilt, you can cut the grid down. If you want to make a larger quilt, you can cut and paste additional quilt rows to the grid by using the extra copies you made of the master quilt grid.

If you are using two different blocks in your quilt design, you must have an uneven number of blocks in each row so the same block is on all four quilt corners. For instance, your quilt grid must be 3 x 3, 5 x 5, 7 x 7, 3 x 5, 5 x 7, or some other odd-number configuration.

If you are repeating only one block in your quilt, you may use any configuration of blocks you'd like.

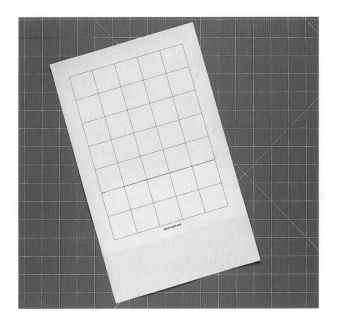

MAKING A DESIGN LAYOUT

WITH YOUR shaded block cutouts, customized grid, and gluestick, you are ready to start playing with quilt designs. Prepare your master grid by putting a small dab of removable gluestick in the middle of each square. This eliminates the need to glue the back of each square and keeps the blocks from sticking to each other and your table as you remove or play with the design. The only place you need to put the glue is on the grid. If you do not have removable glue, don't put any glue on the grid until your design is complete.

Beginning at one corner, start laying one block in every other space. Now lay the second block in the alternate spaces. Do not use the unshaded versions at this point. Keep playing with different combinations of blocks until you find one that excites you. It's that simple! If you want to repeat only one pattern, fill in the grid with one block to get the full effect of your design. It couldn't be easier.

Once your choices are final, go ahead and glue your design in place. Put your leftover blocks back into their plastic bags. You are now ready to make some decisions about colors and fabrics.

Autumn Splendor is made using two patterns, Starry Splendor and Weather Vane. A rich color-family recipe of purples, golds, cinnamons, and greens on cream background prints was pulled from the outer border print. A few changes in fabric usage were made. The center block of each Starry Splendor was cut from an additional cinnamon print instead of Print C and the four corner squares of each Weather Vane block were cut from Print C instead of the background print. These changes are reflected in the colored drawing of the quilt. Blocks were made in pairs from each collection of prints.

CHOOSING COLORS AND FABRICS

IDENTIFYING POSITIONS

How do you know what the different positions are and how you will use your fabric? Fabric usage positions in each block are distinguished by black, dark gray, medium gray, light gray, and white in the shaded drawings and identified in the corresponding block assembly instructions. For instance, all pieces shaded with black in the block drawing are cut from the same print and therefore would be one position. All pieces in dark gray would be cut from a second print, and so on. The purpose of the shading is simply to identify the positions in the blocks. You will choose your own colors to correspond to these positions.

Let's look at the Ribbon Star block below. The star in the center and the four corner squares are cut from Print A (black). Print B (dark gray) is used for the ribbon surrounding the star. Print C (medium gray) is used for the triangles between the star and the ribbon. White always represents the background print. Therefore, you will need four prints in whatever colors you choose for every pair of Ribbon Star blocks you make.

NOTE: *When you are working with two different blocks, the color you choose for Print A in the first block does not have to be the same color you choose for Print A in the second block, unless you want it to be.*

Another important point is that the shades used in the block drawings have nothing to do with value usage in the block. These colors indicate fabric usage only. For example, the black indicated in a drawing does not mean the print you choose for that position must be darker than the light gray or white positions. Do not let this confuse you when assigning recipes to your blocks.

If you look at the two Mill Star blocks shown below, you can see that both blocks use fabrics as indicated by the block drawing but the value usage is different between the two finished blocks. In fact, in the right-hand block below, a black print was used in the position indicated by white in the block drawing.

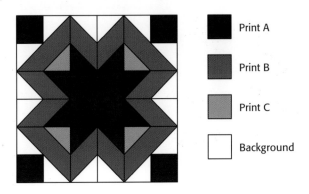

Print A

Print B

Print C

Background

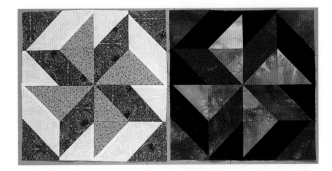

As a further example, study the two Carrie Nation blocks shown on the following page. They are mirror images of each other as far as value goes.

One is blue on white and the other is white on blue, yet both blocks use fabric as indicated by the drawing. In fact, the quilt "Crossword Puzzle" on page 23 alternates these mirror image blocks to create an interesting overall single-block quilt design. You may want to try this positive/negative approach with other patterns.

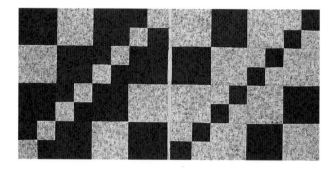

FABRIC RECIPES

YOU CAN use any approach to choose fabrics for a scrap quilt, but there is one tried-and-true method that I use frequently. Select a wonderful multicolor print that you plan to use for the border, and then pull colors from it for the blocks. It has a unifying effect, pulling all the colors together into a cohesive finale. Be sure to buy several yards of this main print. Take a look at "Jewel Box" on page 21. The border fabric was the main print from which the other colors were pulled. But I have to admit the method doesn't always work just as planned. Several years ago I made one quilt that was based on a glorious, brightly colored floral print. I made all the blocks based on colors pulled from that print and then, after the top was assembled, decided the floral just didn't work in the border. Even though I discarded my original plan, the blocks all coordinated beautifully because they had been pulled from that one main print. In the end, I used the floral for the back of the quilt as well as the binding, to great effect.

Even if you have chosen a main print from which to work, it helps to have some guidelines for selecting the rest of the prints to go into your quilt. There are three main "recipe" approaches that I use to choose fabrics for my Scrappy Duos blocks: rainbow recipe, color-family recipe, and mixed recipe. They help bring structure to the selection process.

Rainbow Recipe

A rainbow recipe is truly a scrappy quilt in that every color under the rainbow is used. Every pair of blocks is made from a completely different set of prints for no other rhyme or reason than that you love that combination on that particular day. The result is a lovely riot of color and lots and lots of visual interest. Even though the finished quilt is very colorful and full of many prints, each individual block is made from only two, three, or four prints. This means that each of the different prints is not lost in a muddle but gets to shine in its very own block. Quilts like this are fun to make.

As you can see in the rainbow-recipe Ribbon Star sample, each pair of blocks is made from a different set of colors.

Although many rainbow quilts use a similar background value such as all dark or all light, this is not true all the time. There is no reason why the value of the background print can't change from block to block along with the other prints. A mix of dark, medium, and light background prints would create a fascinating checkerboard look. Look at "Auntie M's First—MDW" (page 27) to see how Merri Wright used the idea of different background values in a rainbow-recipe quilt.

Choosing a rainbow recipe does not preclude having a theme for your quilt. While still using a host of colors, you can employ any number of themes by using all batiks, reproduction prints, jewel tones, children's primaries, thirties prints, or pastels to name a few.

Color-Family Recipe

The second recipe, a color-family recipe, is usually the most comfortable choice. Instead of using any color imaginable, assign a color family to each position in the block. Each time you make a pair of blocks, follow the same recipe but use different prints from the appropriate color families.

For instance, if you decide that Print A=blue, Print B=red, Print C=gold, and background= cream, every time you make a new pair of blocks you will choose a new set of blue, red, gold, and cream prints and use them in the same assigned positions.

Take a look at the Ribbon Star sample shown at top right. I made each block from a different set of prints, but I repeated the same color family in the same position in each block. The scrappiness comes from the variety of prints, not the variety of color.

Mixed Recipe

A mixed recipe uses elements of both color-family and rainbow recipes in the same quilt. You decide how much or how little you use of each recipe.

First, assign a color family to each position that you want to maintain as a constant color. Now identify the other positions as rainbows, or wild cards. For instance in the Ribbon Star sample below, Print A=blue, Print B=rainbow, Print C=rainbow, background=cream. When choosing the four prints for a pair of blocks, blue and cream prints are always in the same positions but the colors of Prints B and C vary.

As an alternative, you can use a color-family recipe approach in all positions of both blocks except one, where you use a rainbow of colors. Look at Kari Lane's "Job 38: 35–36 Lightning Bolts I" (page 26) for an excellent example of this type of mixed recipe. Kari controlled all positions in both blocks with a color-family recipe, except for the pinwheels in the center of the Mosaic blocks, which are made from a rainbow of colors.

Or, for example, you can use a color-family recipe for all of one block and a rainbow recipe for the second. Remember, the degree to which you mix the two recipes is up to you and your imagination.

CHANGING FABRIC USAGE

ONE ADDITIONAL note concerns changes you may want to make to the actual fabric usage given for each pattern. Look at the Ribbon Star block again. What if you wanted to use a fifth print for the four corner squares instead of cutting them from Print A? There is no reason why you can not make such changes yourself. Read the cutting and block assembly instructions for that block to identify which cut pieces go in that position. Then put a stick-on note next to the cutting instruction indicating that you want to cut those pieces from Print D, not Print A.

Or, if you prefer, you can rewrite the complete cutting instructions on a separate sheet of paper to include the changes. All of the cutting instructions are short and simple, so rewriting is not an involved process.

COLORING YOUR QUILT DESIGN

IF YOU need a more visual image of your quilt, glue the unshaded versions of the blocks you have chosen onto a new grid. Then referring back to the shaded version for usage, use colored pencils to fill in the blocks with the recipe you have chosen. This is especially helpful when working with a color-family or mixed recipe because you can preview your idea and make any changes you feel are necessary. It is not particularly useful with the rainbow recipe, because there really is no master color plan to envision.

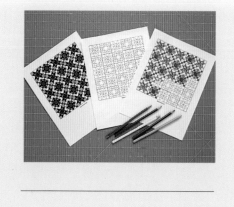

IF YOU ARE NOT SURE *about the colors you'd like to work with, photocopy the unshaded quilt design several times so that you can play with many different coloring ideas.*

Color Cards

If you have decided to use a color-family or mixed recipe, you need to record your assignments. Use a three-by-five-inch card or piece of notepaper to identify your recipe choices for the one or two blocks you will use in the quilt. For example, perhaps you have chosen to alternate the Martha Washington Star block with Outward Bound. Label the first card "Martha Washington Star." Then list the fabrics needed: Print A, Print B, Print C, and background, and the recipe assignment for each. Do the same for Outward Bound on a second card. These color cards are your master guides when choosing prints for each new pair of blocks. Keep each color card with the corresponding block assembly instructions.

You don't need to make a color card for rainbow quilts since each pair of blocks will be unique.

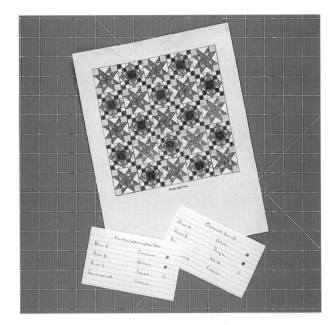

Star Bright Poppies is made using two patterns, Eddystone Light and Double Star Patch. This rainbow recipe quilt is pulled together by the colorful poppy border print coincidentally found in the quiltmaker's stash. You may choose to pick a multicolor border print before selecting fabrics for the blocks. You do not need a colored drawing for a rainbow recipe quilt, as the colors will change from block to block. A single block was made from each collection of prints because the quilt has only nine blocks.

Making Your Quilts

Refer to "Basic Quiltmaking Techniques" on pages 74–83 for basic information on making quilts, including supplies needed, preparing fabrics, pressing, rotary cutting, and finishing techniques. It also includes two techniques that are used in making some of the blocks: add-an-inch bias squares and folded corners. Be sure to read "Basic Quiltmaking Techniques" thoroughly so that you are familiar with the techniques used in this book.

Block Construction

You have designed your quilt, chosen a recipe, made color cards if necessary, and noted any changes to the cutting directions on the corresponding block assembly instructions. Now it's time to start making your blocks.

The process is simple. Turn to the block assembly instructions for one of your blocks. Using your color card, pick a set of prints that matches your recipe. If you are working with a rainbow recipe, simply pull a set of prints following the fabric usage shown in the block design.

You'll notice that no fabric yardage is given. You are making only two blocks from each set of prints, so traditional yardage amounts would be useless. Fat quarters are more than enough for each print used in any of the blocks, with the exception of Print B in Gentleman's Fancy (page 50), which requires ⅜ yard. Unless you make major changes and use one print where the instructions say to use several, you can use a fat quarter as a safe guideline. Cutting is very simple for each print, and you can easily see for yourself how much or

how little fabric you need to meet the requirements.

Wash and press the first set of prints and, following your color card, begin cutting the pieces needed from each print. Then, referring to the appropriate skills in the back of the book as necessary, follow the instructions given to make a pair of blocks from that set of prints.

Small arrows in the assembly diagrams indicate the direction in which to press the seams. Blocks that go together in a nine-patch fashion will have seams pressed in opposite directions from row to row as shown below. When the rows are sewn together, the final horizontal seams are pressed away from the center (heavy lines indicate final seams). In this way, when two such blocks are sewn together they can be rotated so seams will always butt along the block edges.

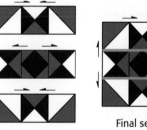

Row seams

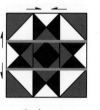

Final seams

Rotate block so seams butt.

Four-patch-type blocks can always be rotated so their final center seams butt.

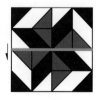

Final seam

Rotate block so seams butt.

It was impossible for me to prepare seam-pressing instructions that would work for all block-pair configurations possible with this book. Therefore, you may want to change some of the pressing directions according to the needs of your particular pattern choices so they butt where they meet along the edges. The considerations I have made for the final seams should help.

QUANTITY OF BLOCKS

SOMETIMES YOU may want to increase or decrease the number of blocks you make from each set of prints. If, for example, you are making a smaller quilt with a 3 x 3 block set, you need only nine blocks for the entire quilt. Therefore, to increase the variety of prints used, you may want to consider making only one block from each set of prints instead of the standard two. It is easy to adjust the cutting instructions by cutting all the quantities listed (but not the sizes!) in half. As you follow the assembly instructions, remember to make half as many units as indicated in each step.

On the other hand, if you are making a very large quilt and would prefer to make four blocks from every set of prints, double the number of pieces you cut from each print. You will make twice as many units as indicated in the assembly instructions.

Obviously, fabric requirements will be halved for a single block and doubled for four blocks. You may want to note any of these changes on a separate sheet of paper.

BORDERS

ONCE YOUR blocks are sewn together to make the quilt top, it is time to make decisions about borders. The samples shown in this book all have simple borders. I find plain borders a nice counterbalance to all of the visual activity in the center. If

you want to make more intricate borders, I suggest you review some of the wonderful books on borders available today. I will review plain borders briefly below.

As a general rule, I like to repeat predominant colors in the borders. If I have chosen a main print as a starting point for my blocks, I will try to use that print as one of the borders. Many times, I like to "float" a more intricate quilt design on a first border of background fabric and then frame it with other coordinating borders. Examples of floating can be seen in "Autumn Splendor" (page 24), and "Jewel Box" (page 21). On occasion, I have found the perfect solution is no border at all. See "Crossword Puzzle" on page 23.

Once you have decided on the number and widths of your borders, you need to calculate cutting and yardage. I like to make efficient use of my fabric. Seams in a border do not bother me in the least. I cut and sew selvage-to-selvage fabric strips into one long pieced border and then cut individual borders from this long length.

For example, if you were adding a 5½" (6" cut width) border to a quilt that measured 60" x 72":

(A) Add: 60" + 60" + 72" + 72" = 264"

(B) Multiply: 4 x 6"= 24" and then add: 24" + 264" = 288"

(C) Add: 12" + 288"= 300" of border

(D) Divide: 300" ÷ 42" = 7.142 strips rounded up to 8 strips, each cut 6" x 42"

(E) Multiply: 8 strips x 6" width = 48"

(F) Divide: 48" ÷ 36 = 1.33 (1⅜ yard)

(G) Add: 1⅜ yard + ¼ yard = 1½ yards for the border

For the example above, you would need 1½ yards of fabric, cut into eight strips, each 6" x 42". Sew the border strips together end to end to make one continuous strip and follow the steps on page 19 to cut and sew them in place.

WORKSHEET FOR EACH BORDER

To determine how much fabric you need:

Add the lengths of the four sides of your quilt.
These dimensions include any borders that are attached
before the border you are now cutting.

_____A

Multiply the cut width of the border by 4 and add it to the
quilt sides.

cut width x 4 + A
=_____B

Add 12" more for margin. This is the length of the long pieced border
you need to make.

B + 12"
=_____C

Divide by 42" to get the number of selvage-to-selvage
border strips you need to cut. I assume 42" from selvage to selvage,
but you may want to change this figure if your fabric is wider
or narrower.

C ÷ 42"
=_____D

Multiply the number of 42"-long strips you need by the cut
width of each strip.

D x cut width
=_____E

Divide by 36" to get the exact yardage you need.

E ÷ 36
=_____F

To allow for shrinkage, add ¼ yard to the exact yardage and
purchase this much fabric.

F + ¼ yd.
=_____G

1. Measure the quilt from the top to the bottom edge through the center of the quilt. From the long pieced strip, cut 2 border strips to this measurement and pin them to the sides of the quilt, easing to fit as necessary.

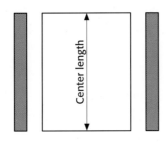

2. Sew the borders in place and press the seams toward the borders.

3. Measure the center width of the quilt, including the side borders, to determine the measurement of the top and bottom border strips. Cut the borders to this measurement, and pin them to the top and bottom of the quilt top, again easing to fit as necessary. Stitch in place and press the seams toward the border strips.

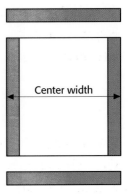

DESIGN SUMMARY

HERE'S A QUICK summary of the process involved in making a Scrappy Duos quilt.

- Decide on the set and size of your quilt.

- Choose which blocks you'd like to try mixing in your quilt. Copy the appropriate block clusters and the master quilt grid several times each.

- Cut the block clusters apart and come up with a design you like by alternating the blocks in the grid. Glue your final design in place on the grid.

- Assign a rainbow, color-family, or mixed fabric recipe to your design.

- Create a color version of your quilt, if you'd like, by gluing the unshaded block clusters to your grid. Following your recipe, color them in with colored pencils.

- Make color cards, if necessary.

- Choose fabrics for each pair of blocks. You can do this on an as-you-go basis.

- Make the blocks following the directions given.

- Sew the quilt top together and add borders.

- Call all your quilting buddies to come see this gorgeous quilt YOU designed!

Do not be concerned that there aren't any traditional quilt plans in this book—this is not meant to be a "pattern" book. Even so, you will find information to help you make any of the quilts and quilt drawings shown in the book. As you browse through the captions in "Gallery of Quilts," you will find the name and quantity of each block used for that quilt, the color recipe used, and the location of the assembly instructions for each block. With this information in hand and the Design Summary on this page, you can turn to the appropriate pages and begin construction of your own version of any particular quilt. You will find similar information with each quilt drawing. Border calculations and construction information is provided on pages 18–19 and can be used to replicate any of the simple borders you see in "Gallery of Quilts."

Scrappy Duos provides information, tools, and twenty blocks so you can plan your own unique quilts. The main purpose of the completed quilts and the quilt drawings is to inspire you with a multitude of ideas to further this end. So take some time to browse through the galleries to gather ideas, see what others have done with the same tools, and become inspired to get started on your own Scrappy Duos quilt!

JEWEL BOX by Donna Lynn Thomas, 1999, Buckingham, Pennsylvania, 80½ x 80½". Quilted by Kari Lane. Thirteen Outward Bound blocks (page 55) and twelve Folded Box blocks (page 49); color-family recipe. Jewel tones pulled from the lively border print dance across the surface of this cheerful quilt. The red squares in the Outward Bound blocks form a diagonal chain that pulls it all together.

PADDLE STAR by Donna Lynn Thomas, 1999, Buckingham, Pennsylvania, 44½" x 44½". Quilted by Ann Woodward. Nine Paddle Star blocks (page 56); rainbow recipe. Sparkly Variable Stars form at the corners where the Paddle Star blocks meet in this bright and colorful little quilt. With just nine blocks in the quilt, only one block was made from each combination of prints.

RISING STAR by Donna Lynn Thomas, 1999, Buckingham, Pennsylvania, 48" x 48". Machine quilted by Kari Lane. Five Mill Star blocks (page 53) and four Mosaic blocks (page 54); color-family recipe. Strong colors such as red, black, and silver always create visual interest. The block interplay is wonderfully enhanced by Kari's superb quilting in silver metallic threads.

CROSSWORD PUZZLE by Donna Lynn Thomas, 1999, Buckingham, Pennsylvania, 48" x 72". Quilted by Judy Keller. Twenty-four Carrie Nation blocks (page 44); color-family recipe. Interesting things happen when you take one block and repeat it with reversed values. Half the blocks are blue on white and the other half are white on blue. The direction of the diagonal design of the block alternates, forming a chain that is white in one direction and blue in the opposite direction. There is lots to keep the eye interested in this two-tone quilt.

AUTUMN SPLENDOR by Donna Lynn Thomas, 1999, Buckingham, Pennsylvania, 90" x 90". Quilted by Judy Keller. Thirteen Starry Splendor blocks (page 59) and twelve Weathervane blocks (page 62); color-family recipe. A lovely, warm chain of gold pulls the eye across this quilt full of the glorious colors of autumn.

MOOD INDIGO by Kari Lane, 1999, Lawson, Missouri, 61½" x 84¾". Thirty-five Card Basket blocks (page 43); rainbow recipe. You can see Kari's spectacular fabric stash reflected in the colorful Card Basket quilt. The mood may be indigo, but quilted musical notes and the use of bright prints on the dark blue background prints are sure eye-catchers that invite you to take a closer look at this exciting quilt.

Kari Lane, her Aunt Jo, and her cousin, Merri, all used the same blocks in their quilts but each used a different recipe. It is very interesting to see how the change of recipe changes the quilt.

JOB 38: 35–36 LIGHTNING BOLTS I by Kari Lane, 1999, Lawson, Missouri, 60" x 84". Eighteen Mosaic blocks (page 54) and seventeen Paddle Star blocks (page 56); mixed recipe. Kari's quilt is proof that quilts do not always need borders. The Paddle Star blocks form flashes of gold that streak across the surface of this stunning quilt while the ever-changing colors of the pinwheels in the Mosaic blocks sparkle and enliven the design.

AUNTIE M'S FIRST—MDW by Merri Wright, 1999, Atchison, Kansas, 64" x 64". Machine quilted by Kari Lane. Thirteen Mosaic blocks (page 54) and twelve Paddle Star blocks (page 56); rainbow recipe. Not only did Merri use a rainbow of beautiful prints in her quilt but she also played with value to create a ring of darker blocks in the center of the quilt. The result is absolutely fascinating.

OF HAPPY X'S AND LAUGHING X'S by Jo Wright, 1999, Steinauer, Nebraska, 65" x 65". Machine quilted by Kari Lane. Thirteen Mosaic blocks (page 54) and twelve Paddle Star blocks (page 56); color-family recipe. Jo made use of strong contrast in her red, white, and blue color-family recipe. There is a strong diagonal design in this beautiful traditional quilt and lots of visual interest from all the different prints chosen. Jo added a randomly pieced blue border to finish her beauty.

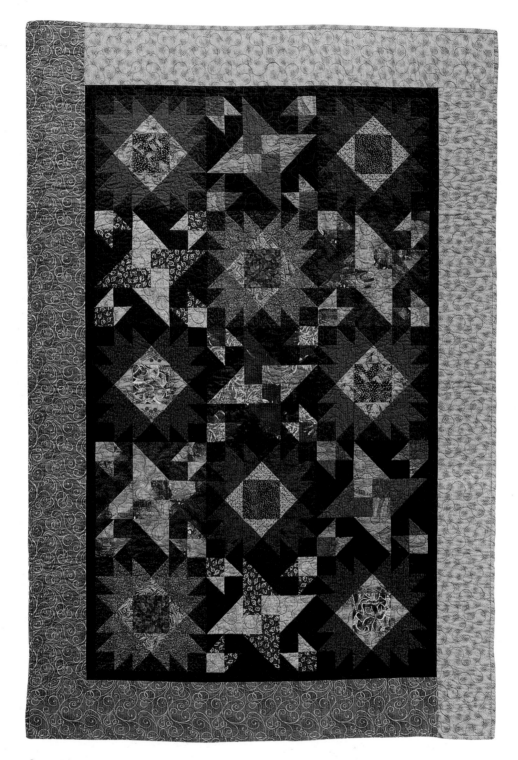

CONTRARY TO THE STARS by Kim Pope, 1999, Buckingham, Pennsylvania, 48" x 72". Quilted by Kris Cooper. Eight Contrary Wife blocks (page 45) and seven Paddle Star blocks (page 56); color-family recipe. Kim's wonderful selection of purple and teal prints strikes a beautiful contrast with the assorted black background prints, making her quilt sparkle with life. The multifabric pieced borders are a delightful finish to this lively and exciting quilt.

PURPLE PIZZAZZ by Ann Woodward, 1999, Collegeville, Pennsylvania, 44" x 44". Five Eddystone Light blocks (page 48) and four Gentleman's Fancy blocks (page 50); color-family recipe. Soft pastels pulled from the elegant border floral evoke memories of times past in this feminine quilt

STAR BRIGHT POPPIES by Donna Lynn Thomas, 2000, Buckingham, Pennsylvania, 52" x 52". Five Double Star Patch blocks (page 47) and four Eddystone Light blocks (page 48); rainbow recipe. Deep, rich prints of all colors mix together in this nine-block quilt. The two different blocks meet at the corners to form a strong and interesting diagonal design. A bright poppy print pulls it all together in the border.

SUMMER SOFT by Ann Woodward, 1999, Collegeville, Pennsylvania, 46" x 46". Nine Double Star Patch blocks (page 47); color-family recipe. Pretty pink chains and soft blue stars grace the surface of this elegant wall hanging. Ann is known for her pastel quilts. Her use of soft reproduction prints here is perfect.

CRAYON BOX by Ann Woodward, 1999, Collegeville, Pennsylvania, 48" x 48". Five Tricky Puss blocks (page 60) and four Folded Box blocks (page 49); rainbow recipe. Colors pulled from a child's crayon box mark a bolder approach for Ann. The "box" effect is successful because of Ann's careful choice of a dark, medium, and light print for each box. The multiprint middle border is a perfect way to revisit the colors from the quilt's center.

CHRISTMAS BAUBLES by M. Deborah Rose, 1999, Lansing, Kansas, 69" x 69". Thirteen Double Star Patch blocks (page 47) and twelve Diamond X blocks (page 46); color-family recipe. Who could resist snuggling under this striking Christmas quilt? The crossing chains of red, green, and purple form strong graphic designs while gold squares seem to lie behind them all. Notice the carefully placed "baubles" in the center of each Double Star Patch block. The pleated red border adds a touch of elegance, and the poinsettias pull it all together to cement the holiday theme.

SCRAP GARDEN by M. Deborah Rose, 1999, Lansing, Kansas, 70" x 90". Quilted by Aline Duerr and Norma Jean Rohman. Eighteen Union Square blocks (page 61) and seventeen Tricky Puss blocks (page 60); mixed recipe. Deb has used a beautiful selection of florals and prints to make her rainbow of Union Square blocks. The Tricky Puss blocks, colored in a recipe of green prints, form a strong chain across the surface of the quilt. Notice the pieced binding. What a lovely quilt for an old-fashioned summer bedroom!

MARIGOLD GARDEN by Cathie Yeakel, 1999, Quakertown, Pennsylvania, 72" x 96". Quilted by Trinity Great Swamp UCC Ladies Aid. Eighteen Poinsettia blocks (page 57) and seventeen Gentleman's Fancy blocks (page 50); color-family recipe. Cathie's great sense of color is evident in this gorgeous quilt. The gold marigold centers sparkle and shine while the soft green Gentleman's Fancy blocks swirl like flying geese between them.

DOLLY'S DUOS by Cathie Yeakel, 1999, Quakertown, Pennsylvania, 72" x 72". Thirteen Martha Washington Star blocks (page 52) and twelve Carrie Nation blocks (page 44); color-family recipe. The cinnamon stars softly connect at the corners while the green Carrie Nation blocks dance back and forth among them. The colors and prints for this beautiful gift quilt were chosen by Cathie and her dear friend, Dolly, who is winning her battle with cancer.

PEACE AT LAST FOR CARRIE NATION by Linda Kittle, 1999, Leavenworth, Kansas, 83" x 83". Thirty-six Carrie Nation blocks (page 44); color-family recipe. The black chain squares provide a striking contrast and vibrancy to the soothing pinks and greens in the rest of the block. The scalloped edge on the quilt is just the right touch of elegance for this lovely old-fashioned beauty.

PRAIRIE HARVEST by Linda Kittle, 1999, Leavenworth, Kansas, 73" x 73". Thirteen Poinsettia blocks (page 57) and twelve Carrie Nation blocks (page 44); color-family recipe. The delicious golds, cinnamons, and browns of a prairie are sure to warm the heart of anyone seeing this quilt. Linda's pieced borders are just perfect.

VICTORIAN WINE AND ROSES by Dee Glenn, 1999, Moorpark, California, 73½" x 73½". Fifteen Weathervane blocks (page 62) and twelve Diamond X blocks (page 46); color-family recipe. Dee chose her colors to coordinate with the beautiful floral border print. While using many different burgundy and green prints in her blocks, Dee chose to repeat the two lighter prints in all the blocks and also repeated the striped pink print to great effect. The result is an elegant quilt that will be delightful gracing any bedroom.

THINKING PINK by Linda Harker, 1999, Leavenworth, Kansas, 74" x 74". Thirteen Ribbon Star blocks (page 58) and twelve Tricky Puss blocks (page 60); color-family recipe. Linda's vibrant pink ribbons are offset beautifully by the light pink chains set on darker greens and blues. In keeping with all these lovely pinks, it's no surprise that Linda made "Thinking Pink" to commemorate the fight against breast cancer.

HUA MEI by Robin Chambers, 1999, Colliersville, Tennessee, 81" x 105". Eighteen Martha Washington Star blocks (page 52) and seventeen Ribbon Star blocks (page 58); mixed recipe. Flashes of color shine and sparkle out of sedate black and gray stars while cheerful pandas look in on this exciting overall design.

STARRY PUZZLE OF MEMPHIS by Robin Chambers, 1999, Colliersville, Tennessee, 50" x 50". Five Indian Puzzle blocks (page 51) and four Starry Splendor blocks (page 59); color-family recipe. Crystalline blue and yellow stars sparkle on this bright and cheerful quilt. A strong and interesting diagonal flows from where the blocks meet creating a very exciting quilt.

GALLERY OF BLOCKS

CARD BASKET
Assembly: page 43
Block clusters: page 84

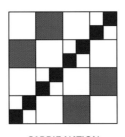

CARRIE NATION
Assembly: page 44
Block clusters: page 84

CONTRARY WIFE
Assembly: page 45
Block clusters: page 85

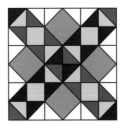

DIAMOND X
Assembly: page 46
Block clusters: page 85

DOUBLE STAR PATCH
Assembly: page 47
Block clusters: page 86

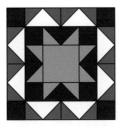

EDDYSTONE LIGHT
Assembly: page 48
Block clusters: page 86

FOLDED BOX
Assembly: page 49
Block clusters: page 87

GENTLEMAN'S FANCY
Assembly: page 50
Block clusters: page 87

INDIAN PUZZLE
Assembly: page 51
Block clusters: page 88

MARTHA WASHINGTON STAR
Assembly: page 52
Block clusters: page 88

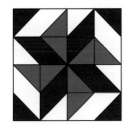

MILL STAR
Assembly: page 53
Block clusters: page 89

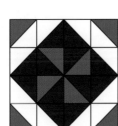

MOSAIC
Assembly: page 54
Block clusters: page 89

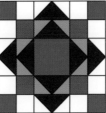

OUTWARD BOUND
Assembly: page 55
Block clusters: page 90

PADDLE STAR
Assembly: page 56
Block clusters: page 90

POINSETTIA
Assembly: page 57
Block clusters: page 91

RIBBON STAR
Assembly: page 58
Block clusters: page 91

STARRY SPLENDOR
Assembly: page 59
Block clusters: page 92

TRICKY PUSS
Assembly: page 60
Block clusters: page 92

UNION SQUARE
Assembly: page 61
Block clusters: page 93

WEATHERVANE
Assembly: page 62
Block clusters: page 93

BLOCK ASSEMBLY INSTRUCTIONS

THE FOLLOWING PAGES provide cutting and assembly directions to make pairs of blocks for each of the twenty blocks in "Gallery of Blocks." A fat quarter of each print is more than enough to make one pair of blocks for all blocks except Gentleman's Fancy. Print B in that block requires ⅜ yard. Don't forget, if you're using a color-family or mixed recipe, make a color card (see page 15) to reflect your choices. You don't need to make a color card for rainbow-recipe quilts because each pair of blocks will be unique.

Cut pieces as indicated in the cutting charts. All dimensions include seam allowances.

In some charts you'll notice a column titled "BS/FC." This column indicates the piecing method for the pieces in the block. *BS* is for bias squares (see page 79), and *FC* is for folded corners (see page 80). If there is nothing in the column, use the piece just as it is cut.

As you begin to assemble your block, please remember that you must trim bias squares to the correct size after stitching the squares together. In the assembly diagrams for add-an-inch bias squares, you will first see the size and number of squares to pair. Then you will see the phrase "Number of (measurement) bias squares." Trim the bias squares to whatever measurement is indicated. For example, if the phrase reads "Number of 2½" bias squares," trim the bias squares to 2½".

In addition, please note the symbols ◻ and ⊠ used in the cutting instructions. The ◻ indicates that you should cut the squares once diagonally to make half-square triangles (see page 78). The ⊠ indicates that you should cut the squares twice diagonally to make quarter-square triangles (see page 79).

CARD BASKET

Block clusters: page 84

TO MAKE 2 BLOCKS

Fabric	No. to Cut	Dimensions	BS/FC
⬛ Print A	4	5¼" x 5¼" ⊠	
	2	4½" x 4½"	FC
🟫 Print B	4	5" x 5"	BS
	2	5¼" x 5¼" ⊠	
	8	2½" x 2½"	FC
⬜ Background	2	5¼" x 5¼" ⊠	
	4	5" x 5"	BS

BLOCK ASSEMBLY

STEP 1

Pair 5" squares.

Number of 4½" bias squares

4   4   8

Add-an-inch bias squares

STEP 2

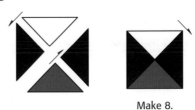

Make 2.

Folded corners

STEP 3

Make 8.

STEP 4

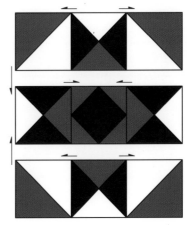

Make 2.

CARRIE NATION

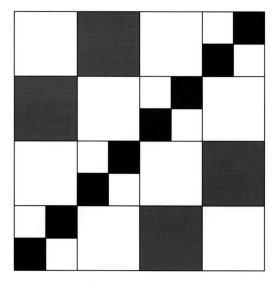

Block clusters: page 84

TO MAKE 2 BLOCKS

Fabric	No. to Cut	Dimensions
■ Print A	16	2" x 2"
■ Print B	8	3½" x 3½"
□ Background	16	2" x 2"
	16	3½" x 3½"

BLOCK ASSEMBLY

STEP 1

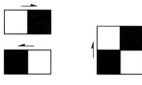

Make 8.

STEP 2

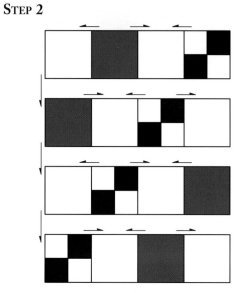

Make 2.

Contrary Wife

Block clusters: page 85

To make 2 blocks

Fabric	No. to Cut	Dimensions	BS/FC
■ Print A	4	5¼" x 5¼" ⊠	
	2	4½" x 4½"	
	8	2½" x 2½"	
	8	3" x 3"	BS
■ Print B	2	5¼" x 5¼" ⊠	
□ Background	2	5¼" x 5¼" ⊠	
	8	2½" x 2½"	
	8	3" x 3"	BS

Block Assembly

Step 1

Pair 3" squares.

Number of 2½" bias squares

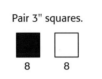

8   8   16

Add-an-inch bias squares

Step 2

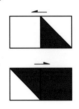

Make 8.

Step 3

Make 8.

Step 4

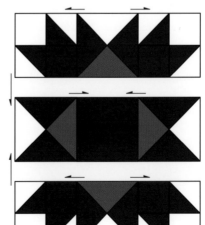

Make 2.

DIAMOND X

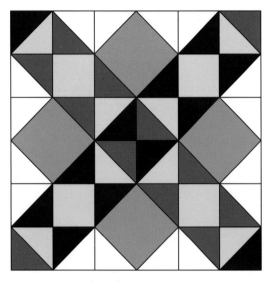

Block clusters: page 85

TO MAKE 2 BLOCKS

Fabric	No. to Cut	Dimensions	BS/FC
■	8	2½" x 2½"	FC
	8	3" x 3"	BS
■	8	2½" x 2½"	FC
	8	3" x 3"	BS
■	8	4½" x 4½"	FC
■	8	2½" x 2½"	
	8	3" x 3"	BS
□	16	2½" x 2½"	FC
	8	3" x 3"	BS

BLOCK ASSEMBLY

STEP 1

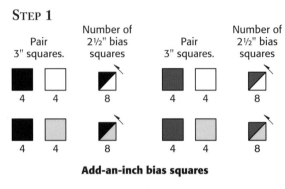

	Pair 3" squares.		Number of 2½" bias squares		Pair 3" squares.		Number of 2½" bias squares
	4	4	8		4	4	8
	4	4	8		4	4	8

Add-an-inch bias squares

STEP 2

Make 4. Make 4.

Make 2.

STEP 3

Make 4. Make 4.

Folded corners

STEP 4

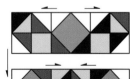

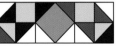

Make 2.

DOUBLE STAR PATCH

Block clusters: page 86

TO MAKE 2 BLOCKS

Fabric	No. to Cut	Dimensions	BS/FC
■ Print A	16	3½" x 3½"	FC
	16	2" x 2"	FC
■ Print B	2	3½" x 3½"	
	24	2" x 2"	
■ Print C	16	2" x 2"	
	8	2" x 3½"	FC
□ Background	8	3½" x 6½"	FC

BLOCK ASSEMBLY

STEP 1

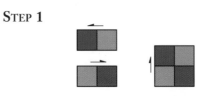

Make 8.

STEP 2

Make 8.

Make 8.

Folded corners

STEP 3

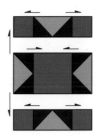

Make 2.

STEP 4

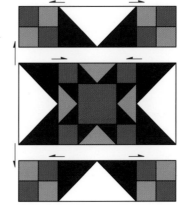

Make 2.

EDDYSTONE LIGHT

Block clusters: page 86

TO MAKE 2 BLOCKS

Fabric	No. to Cut	Dimensions	BS/FC
■ Print A	16	2½" x 2½"	
	8	2½" x 4½"	FC
■ Print B	32	2½" x 2½"	FC
■ Print C	16	2½" x 2½"	FC
	2	4½" x 4½"	
□ Background	16	2½" x 4½"	FC

BLOCK ASSEMBLY

STEP 1

Make 8.

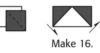

Make 16.

Folded corners

STEP 2

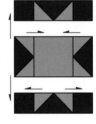

Make 2.

STEP 3

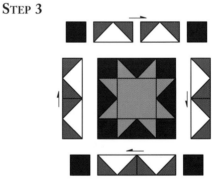

STEP 4

Make 2.

FOLDED BOX

Block clusters: page 87

TO MAKE 2 BLOCKS

Fabric	No. to Cut	Dimensions	BS/FC
■ Print A	16	2½" x 2½"	FC
	2	4½" x 4½"	
■ Print B	4	4⅞" x 4⅞" ◻	
	8	2½" x 2½"	
■ Print C	8	2½" x 4½"	
◻ Background	8	2⅞" x 2⅞" ◻	
	8	2½" x 4½"	FC

BLOCK ASSEMBLY

STEP 1

Make 8.

Folded corners

STEP 2

Make 8.

STEP 3

 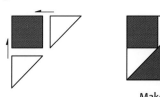

Make 8.

STEP 4

Make 2.

GENTLEMAN'S FANCY

Block clusters: page 87

TO MAKE 2 BLOCKS

Fabric	No. to Cut	Dimensions	BS/FC
⬛ Print A	24	2½" x 2½"	FC
⬛ Print B*	40	2½" x 2½"	FC
	2	4½" x 4½"	
⬜ Background	24	2½" x 4½"	FC

* You will need ⅜ yard of print B for 2 blocks.

BLOCK ASSEMBLY

STEP 1

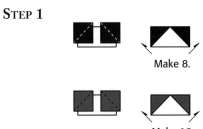

Make 8.

Make 16.

Folded corners

STEP 2

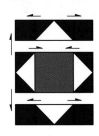

Make 2.

STEP 3

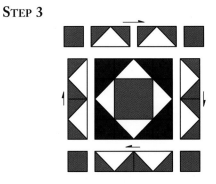

STEP 4

Make 2.

INDIAN PUZZLE

Block clusters: page 88

TO MAKE 2 BLOCKS

Fabric	No. to Cut	Dimensions	BS/FC
■ Print A	16	2½" x 2½"	FC
	8	2½" x 4½"	FC
	2	4½" x 4½"	FC
■ Print B	16	2½" x 2½"	FC
	8	3" x 3"	BS
■ Print C	8	2½" x 2½"	
	8	2½" x 4½"	FC
□ Background	16	2½" x 2½"	FC
	8	3" x 3"	BS

BLOCK ASSEMBLY

STEP 1

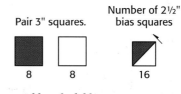

Pair 3" squares.   Number of 2½" bias squares

8   8   16

Add-an-inch bias squares

STEP 2

Make 8.

STEP 3

Make 2.

Folded corners

STEP 4

Make 8.   Make 8.

Folded corners

STEP 5

Make 8.

STEP 6

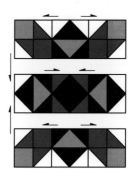

Make 2.

MARTHA WASHINGTON STAR

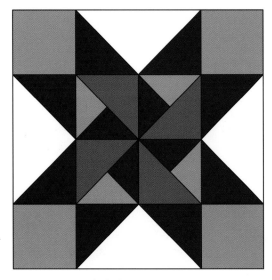

Block clusters: page 88

TO MAKE 2 BLOCKS

Fabric		No. to Cut	Dimensions	BS/FC
■	Print A	16	3½" x 3½"	FC
		2	4¼" x 4¼" ⊠	
▨	Print B	4	3⅞" x 3⅞" ◺	
▨	Print C	8	3½" x 3½"	
		2	4¼" x 4¼" ⊠	
□	Background	8	3½" x 6½"	FC

BLOCK ASSEMBLY

STEP 1

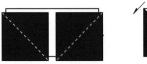

Make 8.

Folded corners

STEP 2

Make 8.

STEP 3

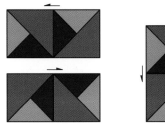
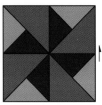

Make 2.

STEP 4

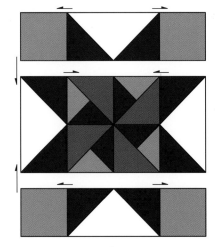

Make 2.

MILL STAR

Block clusters: page 89

TO MAKE 2 BLOCKS

Fabric	No. to Cut	Dimensions	BS/FC
■ Print A	8	3½" x 6½"	FC
	8	3½" x 3½"	FC
■ Print B	16	3½" x 3½"	FC
□ Background	8	3½" x 6½"	FC
	8	3½" x 3½"	FC

BLOCK ASSEMBLY

STEP 1

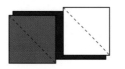 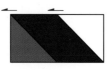

Make 8.

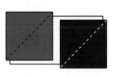 

Make 8.

Folded corners

STEP 2

Make 8.

STEP 3

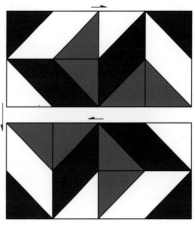

Make 2.

MOSAIC

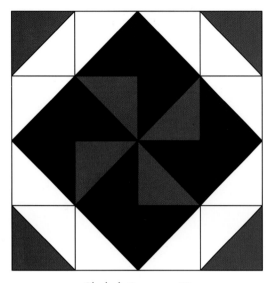

Block clusters: page 89

TO MAKE 2 BLOCKS

Fabric	No. to Cut	Dimensions	BS/FC
Print A	12	4" x 4"	BS
Print B	8	4" x 4"	BS
Background	12	4" x 4"	BS

BLOCK ASSEMBLY

STEP 1

Pair 4" squares.

Number of 3½" bias squares

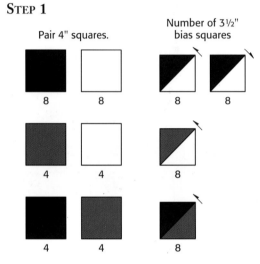

8   8   8   8

4   4   8

4   4   8

Add-an-inch bias squares

STEP 2

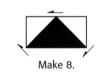

Make 8.

STEP 3

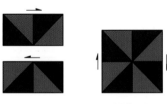

Make 2.

STEP 4

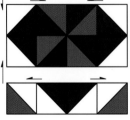

Make 2.

OUTWARD BOUND

Block clusters: page 90

TO MAKE 2 BLOCKS

Fabric	No. to Cut	Dimensions	BS/FC
■ Print A	16	2½" x 4½"	FC
■ Print B	2	4½" x 4½"	
	16	2½" x 2½"	
■ Print C	16	2½" x 2½"	FC
□ Background	32	2½" x 2½"	FC

BLOCK ASSEMBLY

STEP 1

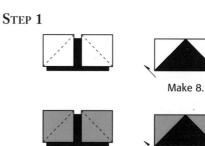

Make 8.

Make 8.

Folded corners

STEP 2

Make 8.

STEP 3

Make 8.

STEP 4

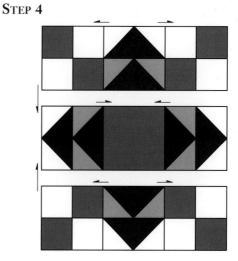

Make 2.

PADDLE STAR

Block clusters: page 90

To make 2 blocks

Fabric	No. to Cut	Dimensions	BS/FC
■ Print A	2	5" x 5"	BS
	4	3" x 3"	BS
	8	2½" x 2½"	
■ Print B	2	5" x 5"	BS
	4	3" x 3"	BS
	8	2½" x 2½"	
□ Background	4	5" x 5"	BS
	8	3" x 3"	BS
	8	2½" x 2½"	

BLOCK ASSEMBLY

STEP 1

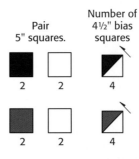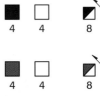

	Pair 5" squares.		Number of 4½" bias squares	Pair 3" squares.		Number of 4½" bias squares
	2	2	4	4	4	8
	2	2	4	4	4	8

Add-an-inch bias squares

STEP 2

Make 4.   Make 4.

STEP 3

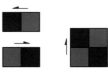

Make 2.

STEP 4

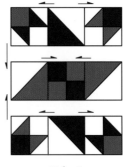

Make 2.

POINSETTIA

Block clusters: page 91

TO MAKE 2 BLOCKS

Fabric	No. to Cut	Dimensions	BS/FC
⬛ Print A	16	2" x 2"	FC
	2	3½" x 3½"	
⬛ Print B	24	2" x 2"	
	8	2" x 3½"	FC
⬛ Print C	24	2" x 2"	FC
	8	2" x 3½"	FC
	8	2" x 6½"	
⬜ Background	8	2" x 2"	
	8	2" x 3½"	

BLOCK ASSEMBLY

STEP 1

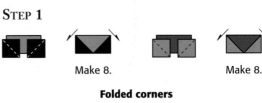

Make 8.   Make 8.

Folded corners

STEP 2

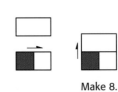

Make 8.

STEP 3

Make 8.

STEP 4

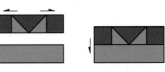

Make 2.

STEP 5

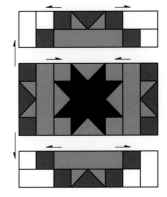

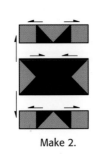

Make 2.

Ribbon Star

Block clusters: page 91

To make 2 blocks

Fabric	No. to Cut	Dimensions	BS/FC
Print A	24	2½" x 2½"	FC
	2	4½" x 4½"	
Print B	4	4⅞" x 4⅞" ◹	
	16	2½" x 4½"	FC
Print C	8	2½" x 2½"	FC
Background	8	2⅞" x 2⅞" ◹	
	16	2½" x 2½"	FC

Block Assembly

Step 1

Make 8.   Make 8.

Folded corners

Step 2

Make 8.

Step 3

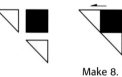

Make 8.

Step 4

Make 8.

Step 5

Make 8.

Folded corners

Step 6

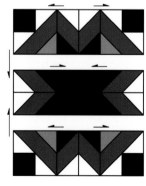

Make 2.

STARRY SPLENDOR

Block clusters: page 92

TO MAKE 2 BLOCKS

Fabric	No. to Cut	Dimensions	BS/FC
■ Print A	16	2½" x 2½"	FC
	8	3" x 3"	BS
■ Print B	16	2½" x 4½"	FC
■ Print C	16	2½" x 2½"	FC
	2	4½" x 4½"	
□ Background	16	2½" x 2½"	FC
	8	3" x 3"	BS

BLOCK ASSEMBLY

STEP 1

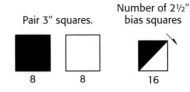

Pair 3" squares.   Number of 2½" bias squares

8   8   16

Add-an-inch bias squares

STEP 2

Make 8.

STEP 3

Make 8.   Make 8.

Folded corners

STEP 4

Make 8.

STEP 5

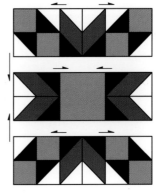

Make 2.

Tricky Puss

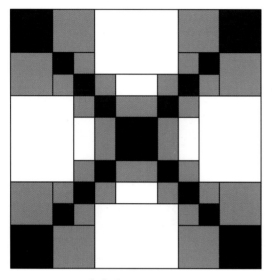

Block clusters: page 92

To make 2 blocks

Fabric	No. to Cut	Dimensions
■ Print A	24	1½" x 1½"
	10	2½" x 2½"
■ Print B	32	1½" x 1½"
	16	2½" x 2½"
	8	1½" x 2½"
□ Background	8	3½" x 4½"
	8	1½" x 2½"

Block Assembly

Step 1

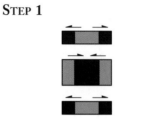

Make 2.

Step 2

Make 8.

Step 3

Make 8.

Step 4

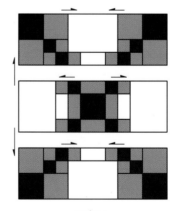

Make 2.

UNION SQUARE

Block clusters: page 93

TO MAKE 2 BLOCKS

Fabric	No. to Cut	Dimensions	BS/FC
■ Print A	4	5¼" x 5¼" ⊠	
	2	4½" x 4½"	
	4	3" x 3"	BS
	16	1½" x 1½"	
▦ Print B	2	5¼" x 5¼" ⊠	
	8	3" x 3"	BS
□ Background	2	5¼" x 5¼" ⊠	
	16	1½" x 1½"	
	12	3" x 3"	BS

BLOCK ASSEMBLY

STEP 1

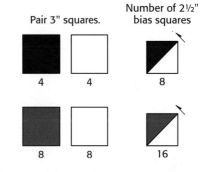

Pair 3" squares.   Number of 2½" bias squares

4   4   8

8   8   16

Add-an-inch bias squares

STEP 2

Make 8.

STEP 3

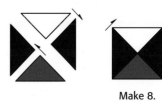

Make 8.

STEP 4

Make 8.

STEP 5

Make 2.

WEATHERVANE

Block clusters: page 93

TO MAKE 2 BLOCKS

Fabric	No. to Cut	Dimensions	BS/FC
■ Print A	2	4½" x 4½"	
	8	2½" x 2½"	
	8	3" x 3"	BS
■ Print B	16	2½" x 4½"	FC
■ Print C	16	2½" x 2½"	FC
☐ Background	24	2½" x 2½"	FC
	8	3" x 3"	BS

BLOCK ASSEMBLY

STEP 1

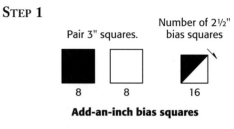

Pair 3" squares.   Number of 2½" bias squares

8   8   16

Add-an-inch bias squares

STEP 2

Make 8.

Make 8.

Folded corners

STEP 3

Make 8.

STEP 4

Make 8.

STEP 5

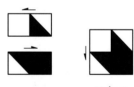

Make 2.

GALLERY OF QUILT DRAWINGS

ON THE FOLLOWING pages you will find twenty full-color drawings of more Scrappy Duos quilts. These drawings are similar to what you will have after designing and coloring your own plans. These drawings are meant to provide you with inspiration and help you get started with the design process. One thing to keep in mind when looking at these drawings as well as any of your own is that the flat color in the drawings cannot possibly reflect the depth, shadings, and nuances possible from actual fabric. Any drawings will be mere shadows of the real live quilt. With that in mind, browse through the drawings and become inspired to create designs of your own!

Use Eddystone Light (page 48) and Weathervane (page 62)
in a color-family recipe.

Use Ribbon Star (page 58) and Indian Puzzle (page 51)
in a color-family recipe.

Use Poinsettia (page 57) and Tricky Puss (page 60)
in a rainbow recipe.

Use Ribbon Star (page 58) and Outward Bound (page 55)
in a color-family recipe.

Use Carrie Nation (page 44) in a color-family recipe.

Use Ribbon Star (page 58) and Folded Box (page 49)
in a mixed recipe.

Use Card Basket (page 43) and Gentleman's Fancy (page 50)
in a mixed recipe.

Use Double Star Patch (page 47) and Poinsettia (page 57)
in a color-family recipe.

Use Martha Washington Star (page 52) and Outward Bound (page 55)
in a color-family recipe.

Use Mosaic (page 54) and Weathervane (page 62)
in a mixed recipe.

Use Union Square (page 61) in a rainbow recipe.

Use Starry Splendor (page 59) and Diamond X (page 46)
in a color-family recipe.

Use Eddystone Light (page 48) in a color-family recipe.

Use Card Basket (page 43) and Mosaic (page 54)
in a mixed recipe.

Use Double Star Patch (page 47) and Eddystone Light (page 48)
in a rainbow recipe.

Use Gentleman's Fancy (page 50) and Mosaic (page 54)
in a color-family recipe.

Use Paddle Star (page 56) and Starry Splendor (page 59)
in a color-family recipe.

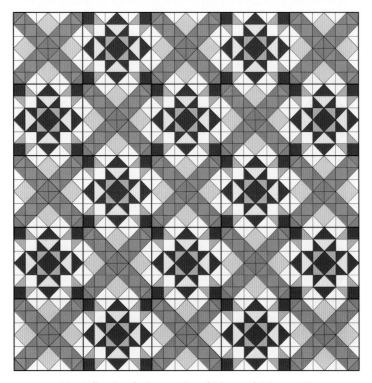

Use Indian Puzzle (page 51) and Diamond X (page 46)
in a color-family recipe.

Use Eddystone Light (page 48) and Outward Bound (page 55)
in a color-family recipe.

Use Poinsettia (page 57) and Union Square (page 61)
in a mixed recipe.

Use Weathervane (page 62) and Paddle Star (page 56)
in a rainbow recipe.

Basic Quiltmaking Techniques

Supplies

The projects in this book are cut using rotary-cutting equipment and pieced on the sewing machine. In addition, there are other items you will need to design your quilts. Listed below are the specific items you will need to work from this book.

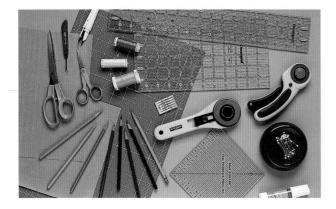

Basic sewing supplies. Keep items such as pins, fabric shears, thread clips, thread, bobbins, sewing-machine needles, seam ripper, and other basic supplies handy.

Colored pencils. Use good-quality colored pencils to color in your quilt designs. Be sure to have a pencil sharpener handy to keep the points sharp. Use a silver or yellow pencil to mark the backs of darker squares for folded corners.

Gluestick. Use a gluestick to paste quilt blocks onto the quilt grid when designing your quilt. Try to find removable gluesticks at an office-supply store. They make it possible to stick blocks in place, and then pull them up and reposition them later as required.

Iron, ironing board, and spray bottle. Make sure the bottom of the iron and the surface of the ironing board are clean. Be sure the iron heats properly.

Lead pencil. A fine-point mechanical pencil is best, but a sharp No. 2 lead pencil works fine, too. Be sure to keep a pencil sharpener handy. You need the pencil to mark the backs of squares used for folded corners.

Paper scissors. Use sharp scissors to cut out the paper blocks for your quilt design.

Rotary equipment. You will need a good-quality rotary cutter, rotary-cutting mat, and a good acrylic ruler with clear markings. Some of the rotary-cutting directions in this book require the Bias Square® ruler.

Sewing machine. This does not need to be fancy; all you need is a machine that goes forward and backward with a fine-quality straight stitch. It should be properly maintained and you should be familiar with its parts and operation. Read your owner's manual to clean and oil your machine regularly as per its instructions.

Super-fine sandpaper. This is a useful surface on which to place fabric squares when drawing lines for folded corners. The slightly rough surface keeps the fabric from slipping when you mark it. For added convenience, glue sandpaper to a piece of cardboard or stick it on self-adhesive needlework mounting board.

Fabric Preparation

Prewash and press your fabrics before starting your quilt. Be sure to check all fabrics for bleeding first. Soak dark and light fabrics separately in very warm water. If the water is clear after twenty minutes, the fabric is ready for prewashing. If not, rinse and soak again. If the fabric still bleeds after several rinses with no sign of letting up, do not use the fabric.

Once fabrics pass the bleeding test, wash them in warm water with quilt soap or plain sudsy ammonia. Use ¼ cup ammonia for a machine or one tablespoon for a sink. Do not use laundry detergent because it can fade fabrics or cause otherwise stable dyes to start to bleed. Dry on low-to-medium heat until damp-dry. Press dry with a hot iron. Gently straighten and refold your fabric from selvage to selvage, as it was folded when you bought it.

Grain Line

There are three types of fabric grain. Yarns running parallel to the selvage are the lengthwise grain. This grain has little or no give. Yarns running perpendicular to the selvage are the crosswise grain and have a small amount of give. Patchwork edges cut parallel to either of these grains are generally considered to be on the straight grain. Bias is any direction other than these two grains, although a true bias runs at a 45° angle to the lengthwise or crosswise grain. The bias grain stretches and distorts easily.

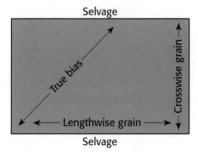

There are two helpful rules to follow when trying to decide which edges to mark on grain.

Rule #1: Place all edges that will be on the perimeter of a quilt block on the straight grain.

Rule #2: Whenever possible, without violating rule number one, sew a bias edge to a straight edge to stabilize the bias edge.

Sometimes, both rules are ignored in favor of design or other considerations. In such a situation, bias edges can be tamed with a little spray sizing or careful stay stitching ⅛" from the raw edge.

Seam Allowance

All the accurate methods in the world won't mean a thing if your sewing is not accurate. Since precise seam-allowance dimensions are included in the pieces you cut, it is imperative that you sew an accurate ¼" seam. If you sew too wide or narrow a seam, the small errors on each seam snowball into frustrating, inaccurate piecing. Ideally, your seams and intersections should fall together into a perfect match.

Conduct a strip test on your machine to test the accuracy of the ¼" seam guide and your ability to use it correctly.

1. Cut 3 strips of fabric, each 1½" x 3". Check the 1½" width of each strip for accuracy.

2. Sew the strips together side by side. Align the raw edges carefully, and sew slowly and accurately by using the machine's ¼" seam guide.

3. Press the 2 seam allowances away from the center strip. The center strip should measure exactly 1" from seam to seam.

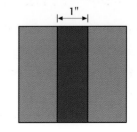

If the center strip is off by just a thread or two, check your sewing habits first. Were the raw edges aligned and did you keep them that way while stitching? Did you sew too fast to properly control the edges while stitching? Do you tend to wander when stitching as opposed to sewing a straight seam? Were the strips cut exactly 1½" wide, or were they just kind of close? These little things are often the source of inaccurate seams. The solution is to slow down. Take the time to be careful and accurate when cutting and sewing.

Your machine could also be the problem. Does your presser foot hold the fabric layers snug enough to keep them aligned? Do the feed dogs feed fabric through without shifting layers? If the machine does not operate properly, get it repaired. The reduction in frustration and seam ripping more than compensates for the effort.

If, despite careful stitching, the center strip does not measure exactly 1" wide, check the seam guide.

Cut a 2" x 6" piece of ¼" graph paper. Put the paper under the presser foot and lower the needle into the paper, just barely to the right of the first ¼" grid line, so that the needle is included in the dimension of the seam allowance. Otherwise, the stitching will decrease the size of the finished area by a needle's width on each seam you sew.

Adjust the paper so it runs straight forward from the needle, angling neither to the left nor to the right. Lower the presser foot to hold the paper in place. Tape the left edge of the paper down so it won't slip.

Check the machine's ¼" guide against the edge of the graph paper. If the guide is the edge of the presser foot, the edge should run along the edge of the graph paper. If the guide is an etched line on the throat plate, the same should be true.

If the edge of the presser foot or etched line does not run along the edge of the graph paper, you need to make a new guide. Stick a piece of

masking tape or self-stick foam along the edge of the graph paper as shown. Make sure it is in front of and out of the way of the feed dogs.

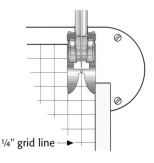

¼" grid line →

Put masking tape in front of needle along edge of graph paper to guide fabric.

Do another strip test to check this new guide. Adjust the tape guide as necessary until you can conduct strip tests accurately several times in a row. If you are using masking tape, build up the guide with several layers of tape to create a ridge that will help you guide the fabric.

BASIC STITCHING

Backstitching. Most, but not all, machine piecing is done from raw edge to raw edge. Backstitching is normally unnecessary because each seam will be crossed by another, securing the stitches in the process.

Rotary-cut pieces. To join rotary-cut pieces, place them right sides together. Carefully and accurately align the raw edges. Sew slowly and accurately with a ¼" seam allowance, keeping the edges aligned.

Matching intersections. The easiest and most accurate way to match intersections is to press seam allowances in opposite directions. Each of the seam allowances forms a ridge, and these ridges can be pushed tightly against each other. This is called "butting the seams." Butting also applies to diagonal seams.

Butt straight seams.

Butt diagonal seams.

Pressing directions. Pressing directions are determined for you and indicated in this book by small arrows in the diagrams.

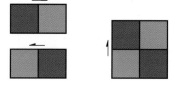

Chain sewing. Chain sewing is an assembly-line approach to stitching. The idea is to save time and increase accuracy by sewing as many seams as possible, one right after the other, rather than stopping and starting after each unit is sewn. When you're finished sewing a set of seams, you should have a long "kite tail" of stitched units connected by small twists of thread. Clip the units apart and press according to the instructions.

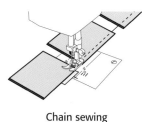

Chain sewing

PRESSING

A PROPERLY pressed seam is cleanly and crisply pressed to one side, without any pleats, distortions, or puckering on the right side. Here a few tips that will help you:

Press, don't iron. Ironing is an aggressive, back-and-forth motion that can easily pull and distort the bias grain or seams in your piecing. Pressing is the gentle lowering, pressing, and lifting of the iron along the straight grain of a seam. Let the heat do the work.

Always press the seam line flat after sewing but before turning. This relaxes the thread, eases out any puckers from the stitching, and smooths out any fullness you may have eased in as you stitched.

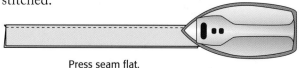

Press seam flat.

Use a dry iron on the cotton setting. Steam distorts. If it's necessary to put a stronger crease in a seam, lightly mist the seam after it is pressed. Then, without any back and forth motion; press the seam dry to form a nice crease.

Arrange the fabric on top (toward which you are pressing the seam) with the open edges of the fabric pieces toward you and the stitched seam away from you. Use the tip of the iron to carefully open the unit, exposing the right side, and then gently press the top fabric over the seam allowance.

To correct mistakes in pressing, return the unit to its original unpressed position and press the seam flat to remove the crease. A particularly crisp seam may need a spritz of water to relax the crease. Once you have removed the original crease, press the seam in the new direction.

ROTARY CUTTING

ALMOST ALL rotary cutting begins with strips of fabric that are then cut into other shapes, such as squares, triangles, and rectangles. To cut accurate strips, it is important to start with a clean-cut edge from selvage to selvage.

Lay the washed and pressed fabric on the rotary mat, with the fold toward you and the selvages at the top edge of the mat. Place the ragged edge to the left if you are right-handed and to the right if you are left-handed.

Lay one edge of the Bias Square along the fold of the fabric. Place a long rotary ruler to the side of the

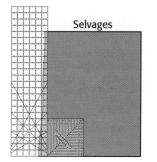

Right-handed

Bias Square so that the ruler covers the uneven raw edges of the fabric and is flush with the Bias Square.

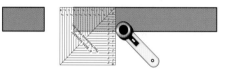

Selvages

Left-handed

Hold the ruler with firm, downward pressure and your fingers spread wide so the ruler doesn't shift. Push the Bias Square out of the way with your other hand. Retract the rotary cutter's safety mechanism, place the blade next to the ruler's edge, and begin to cut slowly away from yourself with firm, downward pressure. Be careful not to shift the ruler out of line as you cut. Start below the fold and cut completely past the selvages at the top to create a clean-cut edge.

Cutting Strips, Squares, and Rectangles

Once you have a clean-cut edge, you can cut strips accurately. If the strip will be cut into squares or rectangles, first cut strips ½" wider than the desired finished size of the square or rectangle. Measure in from the clean edge to the desired strip width. Align one of the ruler's horizontal lines on the fold at the bottom of the fabric to avoid creating a "bent" strip. Cut strips from the bottom to the top in the same fashion as when making the clean-cut edge.

Squares. Cut squares from strips of fabric. First, determine the cut size of the square by adding ½" to the finished size. Cut strips this width. Trim away the selvages and, measuring in from the edge, crosscut the strip into squares the same width as the strip.

Rectangles. Rectangles are cut in the same manner as squares. The cut size is always ½" larger than each finished dimension. For instance, a 2" x 4" finished-size rectangle will always be cut 2½" x 4½".

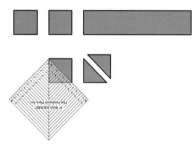

Cutting Right Triangles

There are two types of right triangles that are created by cutting squares differently: half-square triangles and quarter-square triangles. Depending on whether you cut the squares in half or quarters, you can alter the position of the triangles' straight grain.

Half-square triangles. Make half-square triangles by cutting a square in half once diagonally to yield two right triangles with the straight grain on the two short edges.

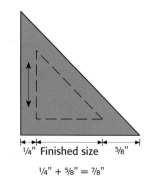

Cut the square ⅞" larger than the desired finished size of the short edge of the triangle.

¼" Finished size ⅝"

¼" + ⅝" = ⅞"

Quarter-square triangles. Make quarter-square triangles by cutting a square twice diagonally to yield four right triangles with the straight-grain on the single long edge.

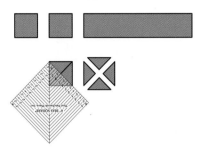

Cut the square 1¼" larger than the desired finished size of the long edge of the triangle.

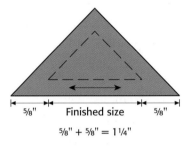

5/8"   Finished size   5/8"

5/8" + 5/8" = 1 1/4"

ADD-AN-INCH BIAS SQUARES

BIAS SQUARES (pieced squares) are traditionally composed of two half-square triangles sewn together on their long bias edges.

} Finished size of pieced unit

Normally, to make bias squares, we cut half-square triangles from squares that are 7/8" larger than the desired finished size of the short edge of the triangle. Unfortunately, once sewn together, the resulting bias squares are usually distorted or inaccurate in size.

The goal of this new construction method is to cut and sew slightly oversized triangles to make slightly oversized bias squares, and then trim the bias squares to the required size as the last step. The result will be perfectly sized bias squares every time with a minimum of extra effort. To do this,

cut half-square triangles from squares that are 1" larger than finished size, instead of the more precise 7/8". Hence the name, add-an-inch bias squares.

For example, to make two bias squares that will finish to 2":

1. Choose two prints for the bias squares and cut a 3" square from each print (1" larger than 2" finished size).

2. Place the two squares right sides together.

3. Cut the pair of squares once diagonally to make two pairs of half-square triangles.

4. Sew each pair of triangles on their bias edges with ¼" seam allowances. Press carefully as instructed on page 77.

5. Trim each bias square to 2½" (cut size = finished size + ½") using the Bias Square ruler. Put the diagonal line of the ruler on the seam of the bias square when you trim each of the four sides.

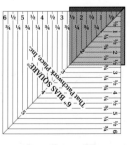

Place diagonal line of ruler on seam line. Trim first two sides.

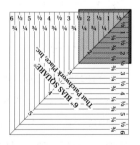

Align desired measurement on previously cut edge and diagonal line on seam. Trim remaining sides.

FOLDED CORNERS

THIS TECHNIQUE has been around for a number of years. In this book, you will find a number of applications of the basic idea used to produce some commonly pieced units. The basic idea is to sew a square of fabric to the corner of a larger "parent" square or triangle, and then fold it over to duplicate a corner triangle.

Use the following simple step-by-step process to make all types of folded-corner units.

1. Determine the finished size of the corner triangle where it falls on the side of the main unit. Add ½" to this measurement and cut a small square this size.

Finished size of triangle is 2".

Finished size of square is 4".

2. Draw a diagonal line on the back of the small square. This line must be very fine and accurate, running exactly from corner to corner. To keep the fabric from shifting as you mark, place the square on super-fine sandpaper. To further reduce shifting, hold your pencil at a flat angle so the point does not drag in the weave of the fabric. Carefully place the small square on the corner of the larger parent unit with right sides together. Pin. Sew on the marked line.

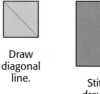

Draw diagonal line.

Stitch on drawn line.

3. Press the small square back over the corner and check it for accuracy. Be careful not to stretch it. It should lie exactly on the corner of the parent unit. If it doesn't, check the accuracy of the marked line or your sewing and adjust as needed. If the square comes up short of the corner, you may need to sew a thread's width

closer to the corner of the unit. If the square is too big for the corner, it may be necessary to sew a thread's width farther to the far side of the line. If there is consistent trouble, check the accuracy of the size of the corner square, the parent unit, the drawn line, or your sewing to find and correct the source of the trouble.

Fold square over corner.

You now have three layers of fabric in the corner. You have several choices when it comes to trimming the fabric from behind the corner triangle.

- Do not trim anything. The corner of the original unit can be used as the sewing edge when sewing the unit into the block. This is okay if you plan to machine quilt through the extra bulk.
- Trim the center layer only. You still have the corner of the original unit as a sewing guide and less bulk to quilt through.
- Trim both layers from behind the top triangle. This is the best option and should be the norm if you are cutting, marking, and sewing accurately to begin with.

Use the steps above to make the types of units pictured here:

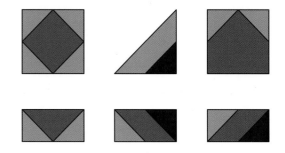

In the directions for making the blocks, you'll find illustrations that designate when to use the folded corner technique. For example, in the illustration below you can see two blue squares slightly offset on top of a pink parent rectangle. The right-side colors are shown so that you know what pieces to use. The squares are offset for illustration purposes only; you would not be able to see the parent rectangle if they were placed directly on top. The dashed line on the square indicates the stitching line. Remember to draw the line on the wrong side of the square and place the pieces together with right sides facing before stitching.

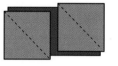

If you have trouble keeping the corners aligned when sewing, try putting a little dab of wash-out gluestick between the two corners that will be cut away. The glue should hold the layers and prevent them from slipping while you stitch.

Quilt Backings

Most of the quilts made from this book will require paneled backings unless you purchase super-wide backing fabric. To figure the yardage for two-panel backing, measure the length of your quilt, add 8" for margin, and double this amount. Divide this figure by 36" to determine the number of yards you need. Add ½ yard for shrinkage.

To figure the yardage for a three-panel backing, measure the length of your quilt, add 8" for margin, and triple the amount. Continue determining yardage as for a two-panel backing.

After washing the fabric, cut and sew it into a two- or three-panel backing as needed. Cut the backing 3" to 4" larger than the quilt top on all sides.

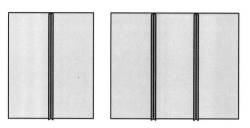

Two ways to piece paneled backings

Basting the Layers

Mark the quilt top with the desired quilting designs and cut the batting to 2" to 3" larger than the quilt top all the way around. Press the prepared backing smooth and tape it, right side down, to a clean, hard surface. Securely tape the sides to the surface every few inches. Tape the corners last. Smooth and center the batting over the backing; then carefully place the quilt top over the batting, right side up. Smooth out the quilt top and pin-baste the "quilt sandwich" through all three layers, always working from the center out.

Using a light-colored thread, thread-baste the sandwich in a 3" to 4" grid, again working from the center out. Baste across both diagonals. Secure the edges of the sandwich with a line of stitches around the edge. Remove the pins.

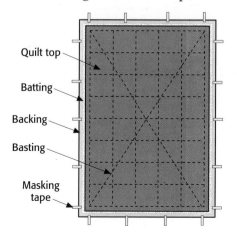

Quilt top
Batting
Backing
Basting
Masking tape

Many machine quilters and even some hand quilters prefer to use special quilter's safety pins rather than thread to baste the quilt sandwich. Place safety pins 4" to 6" apart and remove them as needed while stitching. Some quilters use plastic tacks, such as those used to secure price tags to clothing. They are available at quilt shops or through mail-order catalogs.

QUILTING

QUILTING IS a simple running stitch that goes through all three layers of the quilt sandwich. Stitches are worked from the center out toward the edges. Most quilters prefer to use some kind of frame to keep the layers from shifting while quilting.

Thread a quilting needle (called a Between) with a 12"–18" length of quilting thread. Make a single knot close to the end of the thread. Slip the needle through the quilt layers about a needle's length from the starting point. Bring the needle up and give a small tug to lodge the knot in the layers. Following the quilting marks, sew a simple running stitch through all three layers. This will take some practice to master.

End a line of quilting by making a small knot in the thread, about ⅛" from where it exits the quilt. Take the last stitch between the layers only and run the needle a short distance away from the last stitch before bringing the needle up and out of the quilt. Give a gentle tug, and the knot will slip between the layers. Clip the thread a short distance from the quilt top and work the end back between the layers.

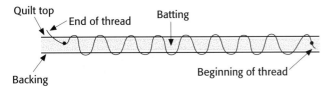
Quilt top
End of thread
Batting
Beginning of thread
Backing

Quilt from the center out to the edges. Once all the quilting is done, remove the interior basting stitches, leaving the stitching around the edge of the quilt in place for the binding.

BINDING

THE BINDING is the band of fabric sewn to the final edge of the quilt to finish it. I prefer to cut and sew cross-grain strips for a double-fold binding. Cut as many binding strips as you did for your outside border.

To make binding:

1. Cut 2"-wide strips from selvage to selvage for standard ¼"-wide finished binding.

2. Join the strips at right angles and stitch across the corner to make one long piece of binding. Trim away excess fabric and press seams open. Use closely matching thread to avoid peekaboo stitches at the seams.

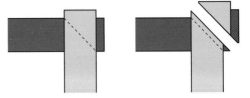

3. Fold the strip in half lengthwise, wrong sides together, and press. At one end of the strip, turn under ¼" at a 45° angle and press.

Fold line

To attach the binding:

1. Baste the 3 layers of the quilt securely at the outer edges if you have not already done so. Then trim the batting and backing even with the quilt-top edges and corners.

2. In the center of one edge of the quilt, align the raw edges of the binding with the raw edge of the quilt top. Leaving about 6" free as a starting tail, sew the binding to the edge of the quilt with a ¼"-wide seam allowance. Stop stitching ¼" from the corner of the first side. Backstitch and remove the quilt from the machine.

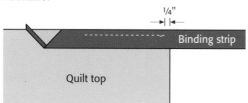

3. At the corner, flip the binding straight up from the corner so it forms a continuous line with the adjacent side of the quilt top. Fold the binding straight down so it lies on top of the next side. Pin the pleat in place. Starting at the edge, stitch the second side of the binding to the quilt, stopping at the ¼" mark on the next corner. Repeat for the remaining corners.

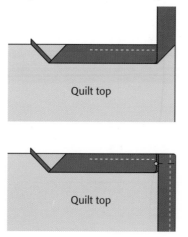

4. When you have turned the last corner and are nearing the point where you began, stop and overlap the binding by about 1". Cut away any excess binding, trimming the end to a 45° angle. Tuck the end into the fold and finish the seam.

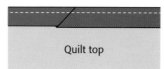

5. Turn the binding to the back of the quilt and slipstitch it to the backing to complete the binding—and your quilt!

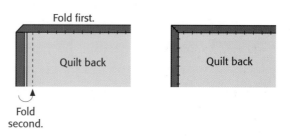

LABELING YOUR QUILT

BE SURE to sign and date your quilt. Labels can be simple or elaborate. They can be handwritten, typed, or embroidered. Be sure to include the name of the quilt, your name, your city and state, the date, and the name of the recipient if it is a gift. Include interesting or important information about the quilt. Future generations will want to know more about the quilt than just who made it and when.

BLOCK CLUSTERS

Card Basket
Assembly: page 43

Run test copy first; adjust light/dark setting as necessary.

Carrie Nation
Assembly: page 44

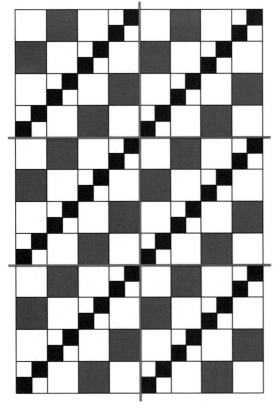

Contrary Wife
Assembly: page 45

Diamond X
Assembly: page 46

Double Star Patch
Assembly: page 47

Eddystone Light
Assembly: page 48

Folded Box
Assembly: page 49

 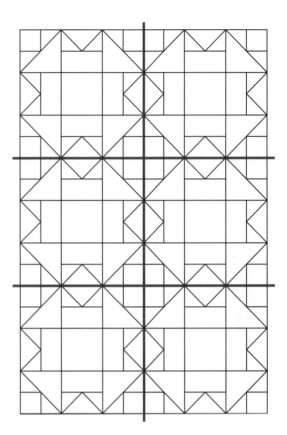

Gentleman's Fancy
Assembly: page 50

 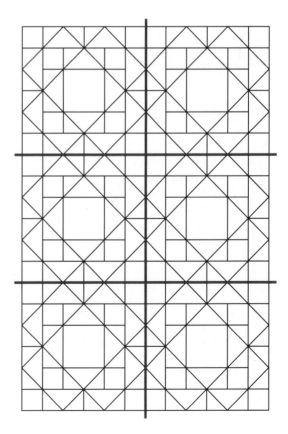

Indian Puzzle
Assembly: page 51

Martha Washington Star
Assembly: page 52

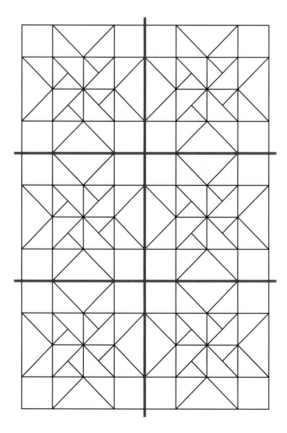

Mill Star
Assembly: page 53

Mosaic
Assembly: page 54

Outward Bound
Assembly: page 55

 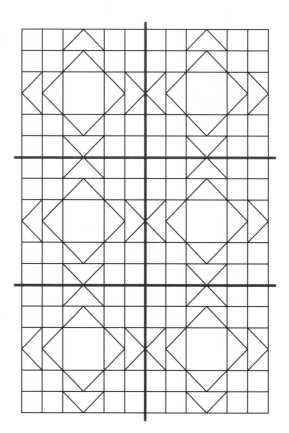

Paddle Star
Assembly: page 56

Poinsettia
Assembly: page 57

 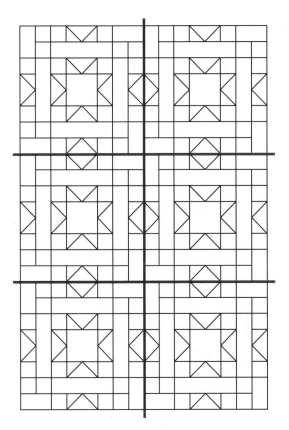

Ribbon Star
Assembly: page 58

Starry Splendor
Assembly: page 59

Tricky Puss
Assembly: page 60

 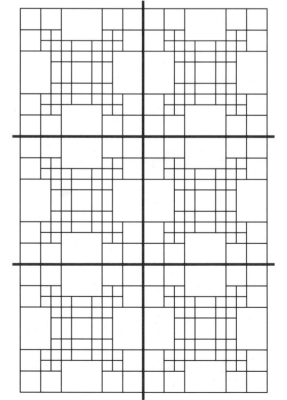

Union Square
Assembly: page 61

Weathervane
Assembly: page 62

MASTER QUILT GRID

ABOUT THE AUTHOR

BORN AND RAISED in southeastern Pennsylvania, Donna Lynn Thomas has had a needle in her hand since she was a little girl. Her mother was a home-economics teacher and her father an engineer. It seems only natural that Donna, with a love for both fabrics and geometry, would take to quilting.

Donna has been quilting since 1975 and teaching since 1982. The introduction of rotary-cutting tools in the 1980s revolutionized her approach to quiltmaking. Since Nancy J. Martin introduced her to bias strip piecing in 1987, she has worked extensively with that method, developing new and innovative ways to maximize precision piecing. In 1995 Donna developed the Bias Stripper™ ruler to use with her bias-strip-piecing methods. She is the author of six other books: *Small Talk; Shortcuts: A Concise Guide to Rotary Cutting; A Perfect Match: A Guide to Precise Machine Piecing; Shortcuts to the Top; Stripples;* and *Stripples Strikes Again!: More Quilts to Make with the Bias Stripper™ Ruler.*

The Thomas family includes Donna, her husband, Terry, and their two sons, Joseph and Peter.

Photo by Kim Gardner Pope

Martingale & Company
Toll-free: 1-800-426-3126

International: 1-425-483-3313
24-Hour Fax: 1-425-486-7596

PO Box 118, Bothell, WA 98041-0118 USA

Web site: www.patchwork.com
E-mail: info@martingale-pub.com

Books from

These books are available through your local quilt, fabric, craft-supply, or art-supply store. For more information, contact us for a free full-color catalog. You can also find our full catalog of books online at www.patchwork.com.

Appliqué

Appliqué for Baby
Appliqué in Bloom
Baltimore Bouquets
Basic Quiltmaking Techniques for Hand Appliqué
Basic Quiltmaking Techniques for Machine Appliqué
Coxcomb Quilt
The Easy Art of Appliqué
Folk Art Animals
Fun with Sunbonnet Sue
Garden Appliqué
The Nursery Rhyme Quilt
Red and Green: An Appliqué Tradition
Rose Sampler Supreme
Stars in the Garden
Sunbonnet Sue All Through the Year

Beginning Quiltmaking

Basic Quiltmaking Techniques for Borders & Bindings
Basic Quiltmaking Techniques for Curved Piecing
Basic Quiltmaking Techniques for Divided Circles
Basic Quiltmaking Techniques for Eight-Pointed Stars
Basic Quiltmaking Techniques for Hand Appliqué
Basic Quiltmaking Techniques for Machine Appliqué
Basic Quiltmaking Techniques for Strip Piecing
The Quilter's Handbook
Your First Quilt Book (or it should be!)

Crafts

15 Beads
Fabric Mosaics
Folded Fabric Fun
Making Memories

Cross-Stitch & Embroidery

Hand-Stitched Samplers from I Done My Best
Kitties to Stitch and Quilt: 15 Redwork Designs
Miniature Baltimore Album Quilts
A Silk-Ribbon Album

Designing Quilts

Color: The Quilter's Guide
Design Essentials: The Quilter's Guide
Design Your Own Quilts
Designing Quilts: The Value of Value
The Nature of Design
QuiltSkills
Sensational Settings
Surprising Designs from Traditional Quilt Blocks
Whimsies & Whynots

Holiday

Christmas Ribbonry
Easy Seasonal Wall Quilts
Favorite Christmas Quilts from That Patchwork Place
Holiday Happenings
Quilted for Christmas
Quilted for Christmas, Book IV
Special-Occasion Table Runners
Welcome to the North Pole

Home Decorating

The Home Decorator's Stamping Book
Make Room for Quilts
Special-Occasion Table Runners
Stitch & Stencil
Welcome Home: Debbie Mumm
Welcome Home: Kaffe Fassett

Knitting

Simply Beautiful Sweaters
Two Sticks and a String

Paper Arts

The Art of Handmade Paper and Collage
Grow Your Own Paper
Stamp with Style

Paper Piecing

Classic Quilts with Precise Foundation Piecing
Easy Machine Paper Piecing
Easy Mix & Match Machine Paper Piecing
Easy Paper-Pieced Keepsake Quilts
Easy Paper-Pieced Miniatures
Easy Reversible Vests
Go Wild with Quilts
Go Wild with Quilts—Again!
It's Raining Cats & Dogs
Mariner's Medallion
Needles and Notions
Paper-Pieced Curves
Paper Piecing the Seasons
A Quilter's Ark
Sewing on the Line
Show Me How to Paper Piece

Quilting & Finishing Techniques

The Border Workbook
Borders by Design
A Fine Finish
Happy Endings
Interlacing Borders
Lap Quilting Lives!
Loving Stitches
Machine Quilting Made Easy
Quilt It!
Quilting Design Sourcebook
Quilting Makes the Quilt
The Ultimate Book of Quilt Labels

Ribbonry

Christmas Ribbonry
A Passion for Ribbonry
Wedding Ribbonry

Rotary Cutting & Speed Piecing

101 Fabulous Rotary-Cut Quilts
365 Quilt Blocks a Year Perpetual Calendar
All-Star Sampler
Around the Block with Judy Hopkins
Basic Quiltmaking Techniques for Strip Piecing
Beyond Log Cabin
Block by Block
Easy Stash Quilts
Fat Quarter Quilts
The Joy of Quilting
A New Twist on Triangles
A Perfect Match
Quilters on the Go
ScrapMania
Shortcuts
Simply Scrappy Quilts
Spectacular Scraps
Square Dance
Stripples Strikes Again!
Strips That Sizzle
Surprising Designs from Traditional Quilt Blocks

Traditional Quilts with Painless Borders
Time-Crunch Quilts
Two-Color Quilts

Small & Miniature Quilts

Bunnies by the Bay Meets Little Quilts
Celebrate! With Little Quilts
Easy Paper-Pieced Miniatures
Fun with Miniature Log Cabin Blocks
Little Quilts all Through the House
Living with Little Quilts
Miniature Baltimore Album Quilts
A Silk-Ribbon Album
Small Quilts Made Easy
Small Wonders

Surface Design

Complex Cloth
Creative Marbling on Fabric
Dyes & Paints
Fantasy Fabrics
Hand-Dyed Fabric Made Easy
Jazz It Up
Machine Quilting with Decorative Threads
New Directions in Chenille
Thread Magic
Threadplay with Libby Lehman

Topics in Quiltmaking

Bargello Quilts
The Cat's Meow
Even More Quilts for Baby
Everyday Angels in Extraordinary Quilts
Fabric Collage Quilts
Fast-and-Fun Stenciled Quilts
Folk Art Quilts
It's Raining Cats & Dogs
Kitties to Stitch and Quilt: 15 Redwork Designs
Life in the Country with Country Threads
Machine-Stitched Cathedral Windows
More Quilts for Baby
A New Slant on Bargello Quilts
Patchwork Pantry
Pink Ribbon Quilts
Quilted Landscapes
The Quilted Nursery
Quilting Your Memories
Quilts for Baby
Quilts from Aunt Amy
Whimsies & Whynots

Watercolor Quilts

More Strip-Pieced Watercolor Magic
Quick Watercolor Quilts
Strip-Pieced Watercolor Magic
Watercolor Impressions
Watercolor Quilts

Wearables

Easy Reversible Vests
Just Like Mommy
New Directions in Chenille
Quick-Sew Fleece
Variations in Chenille